T0102641

THE CANINE COMMANDMENTS

BE HAPPY AND SAFE WITH DOGS

2nd edition

Kendal Shepherd

Illustrated by Anna Currey

5m
Books

First published 2023

Published by
5M Books Ltd
Lings, Great Easton
Essex CM6 2HH, UK
Tel: +44 (0)330 1333 580
www.5mbooks.com

A Catalogue record for this book is available from the British Library

ISBN 9781789181920
eISBN 9781789182156
DOI 10.52517/9781789182156

Printed by Short Run Press Limited, Exeter

CONTENTS

Introduction for parents, guardians and teachers

The first edition of *The Canine Commandments* grew out of a series of lessons I gave to Year 6 students in the primary school my children had attended. Although a lesson is not an accurate description – more an informal information-giving (as well as information-gathering) exercise about dog behaviour and the dog–human relationship. From work completed in class as well as questions asked and answered at home, I gleaned a better understanding of the children's family and friends' approaches to dealing with dogs, as well as what they themselves had learned. By comparing canine and human emotions in similar contexts, empathy for and understanding of both canine and human companions grew.

These lessons culminated in 'Keeping ourselves safe near dogs', a teaching resource published under the auspices of Association for the Study of Animal Behaviour and available from this organisation. The canine commandments themselves are a distillation of what I felt to be the most vital information to get across to children, and of course the adults they would become, all with the intention of reducing dog bite incidents. Apart from the inclusion of current dog bite data in this introduction, showing a worrying increase in incidents, these messages have stayed the same. In this second edition of *The Canine Commandments*, there will be very little change to the 'commandments' themselves.

The most recent studies on the incidence and demographics of dog bites have been carried out by Carri Westgarth and colleagues of the Liverpool University Epidemiology Department. They show that, over the period from 1998 to 2018, hospital admissions owing to dog-related injury increased from 6.34 to nearly 14 per 100,000 head of the population. This increase was largely accounted for by a tripling of bites in adults with the incidence in children remaining the same. Alarming as this increase is, a cross-sectional study in 2017 based on self-reported bites, found a far larger proportion of people reporting they had been bitten by a dog. The owners of multiple dogs were more likely to be bitten, male owners more often than female and by a dog they were not familiar with. Although dog bite injury presented to hospitals is significant in terms of cost to the NHS and its resources, we must assume that the social cost and implications for our human relationship with 'man's best friend' are far greater.

Although one may be comforted by the fact that dog-related injury in children has remained stable, it can still result in life-changing trauma to the child and of course the dog, not least as many are destroyed having bitten. Perhaps contrary to popular belief, the majority of bites to children occur in the home and are inflicted by a familiar dog during interactions initiated by the child and which result in unwitting provocation of, and threat to, the dog. The younger the child, the more likely is a bite to the face or hand. Lack of adult supervision is frequently cited as a contributory factor to such accidents, suggesting that, had an adult been in the room at the time, the bite would not have occurred. Whereas this may well be true for other accidents related to childish exploration, such as those of electricity sockets, cookers or kettle flexes, in human–canine interactions, one cannot be reassured that adult presence will automatically be preventative. Apart from anything else, the speed with which dogs can bite far exceeds human reaction time and therefore precludes effective intervention.

It is therefore essential that adults as well as children become aware of the true nature of dogs and how they communicate. It is often said that dogs view their human family as their 'pack' and treat them accordingly. Apart from the current well-established fact that dogs have no concept of being 'top dog' or of having a 'pack leader', such a view is demeaning to such an exceptionally intelligent and emotional animal, inferring, as it does, that dogs cannot tell the difference between fellow dogs and people. It also belies the thousands of years of co-evolution of humankind and dogs, where both species have become adapted in ways that make it

5

very likely that they will get along with each other. So much so that a pet dog is now considered to be a member of the family, shown the same affection and love as a child. And the emotional bond would appear to be demonstrably mutual. Some argue that the dog–human bond will never be explained fully by the detached rigours of scientific study. As Tina Turner sang in 1984, 'What's love got to do with it?'

So, if a dog bites, what has gone wrong with this unique relationship?

How similar to our everyday expressions of human aggression – in the form of angry words or thrown objects – is the canine growl or the snap? In people as well as in dogs, aggression is an external expression of internal conflict, and arises out of a complex mix of instinctive and learned responses to the environment. It is also a risky strategy in both species, owing to the distinct possibility of being injured oneself during any conflict. Therefore, learning how to live safely and in harmony with dogs, whether in the same house or merely in the same street or town, involves learning about ourselves. This is a process best begun in childhood – although these lessons are of course equally applicable to adults. After all, much of what children suffer at the teeth of dogs is previously created, in both dog and child, by adults.

Increasing a child's understanding of dogs, in order to change the way they behave towards them, should significantly reduce the risk of bites, in much the same way as the Green Cross Code (or 'how to behave around traffic') was introduced to try to prevent road accidents. Any child old enough to understand the significance of the word 'please' is well able to get to grips with the concepts and principles in this book, particularly if they are encouraged to reflect on their own experiences and reactions in various situations, and then try to predict how dogs may similarly feel and respond.

There are marked social similarities between a group of playing children and a group of dogs. Without realising it, children will constantly use reciprocal gestures and facial expressions to initiate, maintain or reject social contact and interaction with each other. In this way, each child keeps a level of social contact within the group with which they feel at ease, and so harmony and stability are generally maintained. Such gestures have nothing to do with indicating rank or social status and are expressed identically by individuals of all social backgrounds. They therefore enable people from all walks of life and experience to communicate effectively with each other and minimise misunderstandings and conflict.

Exactly the same is true for dogs. The concept of a 'pack leader' informing others of what to do, frequently by coercive and threatening means, is unfortunately still entrenched in the minds of certain dog trainers and owners as an essential need for the modern-day domestic dog. This concept was based on the behaviour of captive unrelated wolves, forced into a situation of unnatural stress and social conflict. The more recent finding is that the wolf functions in extended family units, with adult parents and relatives bringing up youngsters in much the same way as in human families. If the 'pack leader' has now become a dubious moniker for the wolf, how much less relevant is it for our pet dogs, to whom we have become 'family'?

Social gestures in both dogs and humans are largely genetically driven, but they require lots of rehearsal in order for individual children and dogs to become 'socially polished'. The extent to which each individual enjoys or can cope with social interaction depends upon character traits as well as their previous experiences. The exact meaning of certain gestures may vary between human cultures and may lead to misunderstanding. In dogs, selective breeding, such as for a short nose, wrinkled skin or staring eyes, may adversely affect the ability of certain breeds to use parts of the body to signal and can therefore limit their ability to be understood by their companions, whether human or canine. One most important anatomical feature, the tail, cannot be used at all if it is removed (thankfully now banned in the UK apart from in certain exempt working breeds) or deformed according to the dictate of human fashion.

Some human gestures do not come naturally, for example, shaking hands and saying 'please' and 'thank you'. They are therefore taught, as soon as a child is old enough to learn, so that they are able to put other people at ease in social situations. A canine equivalent to the human handshake as a social opening gambit is to 'sit to greet'. This is already present in the canine behavioural repertoire but must be consistently reinforced from puppyhood if we want to create a far more pleasing animal than one who continues to jump up as an adult. Both children and dogs learn that socially acceptable gestures are a good way of getting others to be nice to you and achieving what you want out of life! Politeness and manners have become cultural norms for both humans and dogs simply because they are so useful.

The sole purpose of *The Canine Commandments* is to guide children, and, of course, the adults they live with, to interact more safely with dogs and, in turn, minimise the risk of a bite. The 'commandments' are simple to understand and relevant to all children, whether they already live with a dog or not. They are followed by the canine Ladder of Aggression, an illustrated representation of the escalation of gestures dogs will use, if their attempts to keep the peace are ignored or misunderstood. For comparison, description of a human Ladder of Aggression follows. The canine ladder culminates in growling, snapping and biting. No children who have thoroughly learnt and understood the canine commandments should put themselves in a position where there is a risk of being bitten, regardless of a dog's previous experiences of people and the world. At the same time, the dogs they come into contact with will be relieved of potentially unwelcome social pressure and will have little, if any, need to bite. As a result, both children and their canine companions will have considerably calmer and more content relationships.

Each commandment has a multiple choice question to prompt discussion and thereby reinforce learning. There are also learning objectives to set expectations and guide progress.

I was indebted to the late Victor Ambrus for his humorous yet accurate interpretation and illustration of the text in the first edition of the Canine Commandments. I am now very grateful to, and equally delighted to have been able to collaborate with, illustrator Anna Currey and have her beautifully drawn and intuitive work to accompany and embellish the text for this second edition.

Further illustrative contribution has been provided by Matt Black's poem 'How to help dogs avoid going up ladders' – a succinct depiction of the Ladder of Aggression in verse form!

NB The pronoun 'he' is used throughout when referring to dogs for simplicity and clarity as opposed to 'he/she' or 'they'.

Safety first

- **Never** imagine 'my dog will always be good' or 'my dog would never bite'.

- Do not let your dog off lead near deer, sheep or any farm animals.

- Do not let your dog off lead near traffic.

- Make sure your garden gate is secure and kept shut.

- Do not intervene in a dog fight.

- Do not argue or fight in front of your dog.

- If your dog seems ill or in pain, or his behaviour suddenly changes in any way, consult a vet immediately.

Being cross does not make you the boss

1

Although all our pet dogs are descended from the wolf, the dogs we know today no longer live in packs like wolves do. Instead of hunting for a living, the domestic dog has developed as a scavenger of waste that humans throw away.

We used to think that wolves used aggression to fight their way to the top of their pack, but we now realise that the leaders of the pack are simply parents and related wolves who bring up their youngsters in much the same way that human parents and guardians do with their children. One of the reasons we get along so well with dogs is that they are very much like us and need to live as we do – as a family or in a group of friends.

Wolves in the wild communicate with each other all the time using body language to avoid the need to fight and possibly injure each other. They join forces and cooperate to hunt their prey when they are hungry.

Although dogs still very much enjoy chasing things, such as balls, sticks and rabbits, they no longer have to work together to kill and eat what they chase. If a group of dogs run together chasing the same thing, it is because it is an enjoyable and sociable thing to do, in much the same way as playing a game of football, rather than the means of getting dinner.

Dogs are the same as wolves and do not use aggression to make themselves the boss. In fact, they have no idea of what being the boss actually means. Unfortunately, however, many people still believe that an angry and aggressive dog is trying to be bossy and be the 'top dog'. They also believe that in order to make themselves 'the boss', they have to behave in a bossy and aggressive manner towards their dogs. This is not only untrue but extremely dangerous.

If dogs or people get angry and aggressive, it is often because they feel threatened. It is not because they are 'the boss', nor does it make them be 'the boss'.

Imagine yourself in a dog's position. If someone continues to shout or be angry with you, despite your saying sorry or trying to calm him or her down, you will eventually feel you need to be angry in return. Whether you win your argument or not will depend upon what the other person decides to do. He or she may change their mind and agree with you or they may continue to argue and fight. Whatever the eventual result, being angry does not make either person 'the boss'.

A truly trustworthy and reliable leader is actually a very calm and confident individual who very rarely has to get cross or aggressive with anyone. People agree with them simply because they have very good ideas and explain them clearly.

The best way for your dog to think that you are also a good leader and can be trusted to make the right decisions, is to remain very calm when you are with him and not to play with him just because he seems to want to. Instead, you must show him clearly what you need him to do without getting angry. If we get cross, a dog will automatically think that we are not reliable or trustworthy. They will also become upset and anxious and may even feel the need to defend themselves by growling and biting.

Q How do you think you should control a dog?

A
a) By shouting and scolding if they disobey?
b) By nagging?
c) By asking them nicely?
d) By showing clearly what you want them to do first?

(Correct answer on page 64.)

Any dog may bite if he feels in danger

2

You may have seen grown-ups getting angry with a dog and pushing or pulling a dog into doing what they want him to do. **Do not copy them!**

Trying to force dogs to do something they do not want to do is a very common reason why dogs bite us. It also explains why the hand or arm is the most frequently bitten part of our bodies.

Dogs do not start out wanting to bite us but the way we sometimes behave makes them feel in danger. In exactly the same way, there may be times when you have an argument with a friend or brother or sister and end up having a fight. You did not want it to end up this way and would have preferred for your friend or brother to agree with you instead.

We have words and fists to argue and fight with. Dogs have growls and **teeth**.

Dogs often feel they have to bite when we accidentally misunderstand what they are trying to tell us with their body language.

We are able to say with words, 'Stop that. I don't like it', and most of the time we are understood by people around us without having to get upset or angry.

Dogs use their bodies to 'speak' to other dogs and us. If a dog walks away from you, he is simply saying 'I feel a bit worried being close to you'. If he turns his head away as you try to put his collar on or pull him off the sofa, he is saying 'You are making me feel worried and threatened'.

If you walk towards him to try to make him come to you or continue to pull him, you are 'starting an argument' as far as the dog is concerned, which may well end in tears or worse.

The Canine Commandments

If we want to get on well with our dogs, we must never threaten them or make ourselves appear dangerous to them.

Whether a dog feels in danger or not also depends upon what has happened to him in the past and how used to things around him he is. Although we know that trains, planes, people with funny hats on, the postman and the vet are not dangerous, we cannot assume that our dogs also know this.

In much the same way as people hate going to the dentist, because they are afraid that it will hurt, dogs become afraid of things they think may hurt them. The fact that a vet does not want to hurt a dog makes no difference to what the dog thinks. Quite simply, if a dog cannot run away when he is frightened, because he is trapped in a room or on lead, he may well bite. Dogs need to be taught that the world and things in it are nice. If they are given goodies while being patted and hugged by all sorts of different people, they will learn to enjoy this attention. If hands are used to reward rather than punish them, then hands become good news rather than bad.

Q   What do you think might make a dog feel frightened and in danger?

A   a) Fireworks and thunderstorms?
    b) Going to the vets and having an injection?
    c) Being scolded or smacked?
    d) Seeing and hearing people arguing or fighting?
    e) Meeting a stranger?

(Correct answer on page 64.)

Never hit or kick a dog

3

There are two main reasons why people try to control and discipline a dog using their hands or feet. We either use them to force dogs to do things we want them to or to stop them doing things we don't want them to do.

Often, we simply lose our temper when dogs annoy us and lash out without thinking. We may push a dog to sit or lie down if he hasn't done what he's told or smack a dog for chewing our shoes or for weeing in the sitting-room. We may not actually hit a dog but instead, use the threat of a raised hand or foot to say to the dog, 'Do it or else!' or 'Don't you dare!'.

Punishment is unfortunately very much part of the way we humans deal with each other. We think that if we threaten a person with going to prison, or actually send them to prison, it will, for example, teach them not to steal cars in the future. Also, we assume that dogs, as well as people, automatically know the difference between right and wrong.

There is very little evidence to show that this approach is effective with people, let alone with dogs. Punishment for both people and dogs ends up as being a 'tit for tat' system – You've done something horrid to me, I'm angry so I'm going to do something horrid to you back – rather than teaching what should be done instead of being 'bad'.

By punishing dogs when we are angry, a dog may learn only that hands, feet and angry human voices are dangerous and that they might get hurt. If a dog expects danger, he may bite.

The only lesson a dog is ever likely to learn if we hit them is that we ourselves might become dangerous at certain times and should be avoided at all costs. He certainly does not learn that bones should be chewed rather than shoes and that he should wee in the garden in future rather than indoors.

21

The Canine Commandments

You must remember that the next time you want to walk up to a dog and stroke him because you are happy and pleased rather than cross, how is he supposed to know the difference? If you or anyone else ever teaches a dog that hands or feet are 'bad news' and might hurt him, then he may end up wanting to bite them all the time.

Q Why do you think anyone would hit or kick a dog?

A a) They are angry about something the dog has done and lose their temper?
b) They want to stop the dog doing the 'bad' thing again in the future?
c) They are frightened if a dog comes too close to them?
d) For fun?

(Correct answer on page 64.)

Do not touch a dog you don't know

4

Although we may like dogs and want to be friendly towards them, what we do to try to be friendly may be looked on very differently by a dog. A hug and a kiss from your mum and dad or a friend is an enjoyable experience. But you would not want to be kissed, hugged or even touched by everyone, particularly if you don't know them.

Dogs are exactly the same. If a dog has not yet met a person who looks, sounds and smells like you do, or if he remembers something nasty about someone who looks, sounds or smells like you, he will not want you to touch him. He may just turn his head away or decide to walk away from you. He may, however, think that snapping at you or biting is the safest thing to do.

Never go up to a dog tied up in the street and touch him even if he looks friendly and as if he is pleased to see you. It is always safest to walk past calmly without staring at the dog. If a dog is being walked by his owner, again you must walk calmly and slowly towards them and only greet the dog if the owner says that you can. Keep your arms by your

side, offer the back of your hand for the dog to sniff and keep your voice low and soothing. Never pat or try to hug a dog.

Do not assume that patting and hugs, or even being looked at, are things that dogs automatically enjoy. The excitement dogs may show when we approach them is their way of saying that they do not want to harm us and certainly do not want us to harm them. We should think of it as meaning 'Please don't threaten me' rather than 'Please hug and pat me'.

Dogs do however enjoy knowing exactly what they are supposed to do. Asking a dog to sit and giving him a food reward is a much better way of saying 'Hello' than patting him.

Q What would you do if you saw a dog tied up outside a shop?

A
a) Go up to stroke and pet the dog?
b) Run past him?
c) Speak to him but keep your distance?
d) Ignore him and walk past slowly?

(Correct answer on page 65.)

Do not tease or deliberately excite a dog

5

What do we mean by the word 'tease'? Whether you are teasing a friend, your sister or brother or your dog, teasing involves holding onto something on purpose, something you know that they want.

You may be teasing a friend by saying 'I know something you don't know!' or your brother by refusing to share your sweets with him, or your dog by showing him his ball and then not letting him have it.

To a certain extent, training a dog or your younger brother involves a little 'teasing', and we use what we know dogs and people want, to teach them things. The dog can have the ball he wants as long as he sits nicely first and your brother needs to learn to say 'please', if he wants one of your sweets.

What we must not do, however, is keep either your dog or brother waiting so long that they become very excited, upset or angry. It may seem like fun to work a dog up into excitement, particularly when they are puppies, but you will not teach the right lessons if you do. It may even be dangerous to you when they grow into much bigger dogs.

No-one can think clearly when they are over-excited or angry. Instead of learning to sit calmly for a ball, the dog may jump up or even grab your hand or arm instead of the ball. Your brother may burst into tears or try to hit you. On the other hand, a calm dog, or brother for that matter, very rarely causes us any trouble.

One of the times that dogs often learn to behave in an excited manner is when we come home and they seem to want to say hello to us. Such excitement may make us feel that our dogs love us and we automatically want to hug and pat them. However, attention from us when they

27

are excited accidentally teaches our dogs that excitement is a good thing.

If you do not mind your dog jumping up, scratching you and putting muddy paws all over you then by all means continue to say hello when he is excited. But you will create behaviour that is unpleasant and may be scary for others. It may even endanger your dog's life as dogs are not allowed by law to hurt or even to frighten people.

If, however, you would prefer your dog to be calm and polite, then you must turn away and ignore excited greetings. Simply do not say hello until a dog is calm and quiet and will sit when you ask him to.

Q How can you tell if a dog wants to play?

A
a) He runs around with a toy in his mouth?
b) He barks at you while standing over a toy?
c) He's lying in his bed with a toy?

(Correct answer on page 65.)

Dogs do not know the difference between right and wrong

6

We, as humans, are taught very early in our lives what is considered to be 'good' behaviour and what is thought to be 'bad'. We are taught to say please and thank you, to greet one another politely, and that things need to be paid for rather than stolen. We should also learn that it is better to be nice and kind to other people rather than being rude or trying to hurt them. Through this teaching, we develop an idea of what is 'right' (or 'good'), and 'wrong' (or 'bad').

If a dog chews up our shoes, steals food from the fridge or bites the postlady, we are all in agreement that this is 'bad' behaviour. But does the dog know that it is 'wrong' to do these things? At other times, we think that our dogs have been 'good', maybe because they performed particularly well in training class, or have waited until we get home and go for a walk before having a wee or because they come running straight back to us in the park as soon as we call them. But how do they know that these are the 'right' things to do? Do they think of them as 'right' at all?

In other words, what does 'right' and 'wrong' mean if you happen to be a dog? The reality is that dogs have simply no idea of our human concepts of right or wrong and certainly do not choose what to do based on whether we think their behaviour is good or bad.

All they are thinking is that some things, like chasing balls or rabbits, are exciting and some things are boring, like walking to heel or staying at home alone. Things they do may also seem to be safe, like having a wee in the sitting-room or chewing shoes when they are alone, or dangerous, like having a wee in the sitting-room or chewing shoes if someone catches them at it.

In other words, a dog decides what to do based on what usually happens afterwards, rather than whether he thinks he is being good or bad. If we are not very careful, by getting angry we may actually teach our dogs that it is safer to run

away from us and chase rabbits and to wait until we have gone out to wee or chew things in the house. Instead, what we should be teaching is that it is always safe, exciting and rewarding to come back to us and to wee and chew where and what we want.

What a dog views as safe, exciting and rewarding will then fit in nicely with what we consider to be 'good'.

Unfortunately for dogs, they are very good at looking as if they know they have done something wrong when we are angry with them. They may crouch down, lay

their ears back and tuck their tail tightly under their tummy or they may even run away from us. But all they are really saying is 'Please calm down!' not that they know they are guilty of a crime or have been 'bad'.

If you get angry with a guilty-looking dog, all that you will teach him that it is very dangerous to chew or wee when you are around. He will therefore learn that he must wait until you are not there to chew or wee in peace rather than that chewing or weeing is 'wrong'. You may even teach him to bite you.

Q Do you think a dog knows if he's been bad?

A a) Yes
b) No

(Correct answer on page 66.)

Behaviours that dogs enjoy will be repeated

7

Anything a dog does that has a good outcome for him will be repeated, such as walking by your side in exchange for a food treat or bringing a ball back to be thrown again for him. However, what you look and sound like must stay the same, regardless of where you are, if you want your dog to continue to behave in the same way.

If the sound of a dog's name and the sight of a beckoning hand always mean, 'Food available if you run in this direction', then a dog will become very obedient when called. For a dog to really believe in this 'good news', then you must practise everywhere you expect the dog to obey you. If food only appears in training class or in the kitchen but not in the garden or park, then your dog will only believe you are worth obeying in training class or the kitchen.

If a dog is called angrily, with a frown and pointed finger rather than a jolly voice, a smile and wave, and then gets a smack when he comes because he has 'done something wrong', he may well decide, very sensibly, to run away from you instead next time. Your body must always look like good news if your dog is really to trust and believe in you.

We often assume that dogs will do as we want just because we will be happy and praise them. But our own pleasure does not necessarily matter to a dog. Dogs of course want to be happy, as we do, and, like us, will do things to create a feeling of happiness. But problems arise when what makes a dog happy, and what makes us happy, differ.

A dog may enjoy chewing your shoes, but is this what you are happy with? We may enjoy patting a dog on the head to praise him, but is this what he would like the best? A chew toy stuffed with food will give your dog pleasure and you the chance to praise your dog for chewing the right thing rather than getting cross with him.

To train your dog properly, always consider what makes him happy as well as yourself. Let him have what makes him happy as a result of doing something for you. If a dog gets what he wants when we are pleased with him, then he will be happy to please us.

The aim of any relationship between a dog and a person is that both of you should be happy at exactly the same time!

Q How do you know when a dog is enjoying himself?

A When he is:
a) Chasing a ball?
b) Eating?
c) Chewing his bone?
d) Chewing your shoes?
e) Asleep in his bed?

(Correct answer on page 66.)

Dogs must be taught what you want them to do and they must choose to do it

8

Many dogs, when introduced to our houses and the way we live, whether as a puppy or adult, are given the idea that they can do exactly as they please until they do something that makes us angry.

They are allowed to roam all over the house until they wee in the bedroom and then they are confined downstairs. They are allowed to jump up to say hello until they grow bigger and hurt someone and then they are smacked for jumping up.

Instead of showing them exactly what we want them to do right from the start, we wait until they do something wrong and then we get cross with them. This is, quite simply, a very inefficient, upsetting and stressful way to teach or learn anything.

Imagine if your teacher, instead of explaining how to do a sum or spell a particular word, just shouted at you or hit you for every mistake. Would you enjoy being at school? Would you enjoy learning? Would you in fact learn anything at all? However horrible this sounds, this is exactly what many dogs have to put up with every day.

We all know what we don't want dogs to do. We know that we don't want them to bite people, they shouldn't run away in the park, we don't want them to chew our belongings and they certainly shouldn't use the sitting-room as a toilet. But are we doing enough to show them what we do want? Have we even decided what we want them to do?

Before any dog can become 'obedient', we must decide exactly what we do want them to do – not just what we don't want them to do.

We must then make what we want them to do more exciting, safe and rewarding than anything else. Running towards you when you call or having a wee in the garden rather than indoors, will be both safe and fun for your dog if you give a food treat or a toy as a reward.

If we have enough patience and take the time to correctly show them what we want them to do, dogs will then choose for themselves to listen to us and to do as we ask.

Q What is the difference between an obedient dog and a well-behaved dog?

A a) An obedient dog does what he is told
   b) A well-behaved dog is good without being asked
   c) No difference

(Correct answer on page 67.)

Do not take anything away from a dog

9

Whatever a dog has in his mouth, he must choose to give it to you rather than you try to take it away by force.

Dogs have evolved as scavenging animals, which have in the past needed to guard food from others in order to survive. They are therefore much more selfish than we would often like them to be and guarding behaviour can be very important to them.

We may guard something by telling people to stay away or putting a 'KEEP OUT!' sign up on the door of our bedroom or garden gate. Dogs can only do it by holding on to an object, walking away from us, trying to hide and growling.

Dogs often seem to steal our favourite or most useful things. This is because doing so always seems to get us the most excited and results in dogs getting lots of attention from us. Socks, pairs of knickers, your toys, tea towels and the TV remote control are often the best bet as far as a dog is concerned!

If you follow your dog to try to get the stolen object back, not only will he think you are joining in a chase game but he may begin to feel threatened. This is particularly true if your dog tries to hide under a table or in a corner. What may dogs do if they are feeling threatened and trapped? They might **bite!**

Your dog must always be given a very good reason to drop what he has in his mouth. If coming to you always means he gets a tasty piece of food in exchange, he will love running towards you. If opening his mouth to drop what is inside it means the food gets even tastier, he will love to bring things to you and drop them.

If you are angry and chase him, however, he may learn that he has to bite you.

Q What should you do to make a dog drop what he has in his mouth?

A a) Chase and shout at him to leave it?
b) Try and pull it away?
c) Offer him a tasty treat in exchange?
d) Ignore him?

(Correct answer on page 68.)

Do not take anything away from a dog

When dogs are being 'bad', they need the most help, not the most punishment

10

Whenever a dog does something 'bad', in reality all they have done is upset us. Looking at it the other way around, if we are not upset by what dogs do, then we do not consider their behaviour to be bad.

Your mum may hate your dog barking all the time but the old lady who lives on her own down the road may feel very safe if her dog barks a lot whenever someone passes by or comes to the door. Although an aggressive dog is thought to be 'dangerous' and 'bad', many people like their dogs to be 'protective' of them and their property.

What is the difference between being protective and aggressive if you are a dog? Very little, most of the time! But we as humans like it sometimes and reward it and hate it at other times and try to punish it. This can be very confusing if you happen to be a dog.

All the things that dogs do are the obvious choices as far as they are concerned. Although we may think they are being bad or naughty, they are likely to be thinking:

- 'That postman looks dangerous, I must chase him away.'

- 'That rubbish bin smells great. I must tip it over and find out what's inside.'

- 'My bladder's full, it's raining and no-one's looking, so I'll just nip behind the sofa.'

So, we must help dogs to avoid doing things that upset us and make us angry, rather than simply calling them 'bad' dogs, punishing them and expecting them to automatically understand what we want. The truth is that the worse a dog behaves, the harder he is finding it to make the 'right' decision from our point of view.

The same is true for people. Some of you will be very good at sums and spelling but hopeless when it comes to getting out of bed on time and keeping your room tidy. Others may be able to remember football scores, the rules of cricket and how to play chess but have great trouble sitting still and paying attention in class. We all need a bit of extra help sometimes and some people simply need more help than others to get certain things right.

We must therefore think how **easy** or **difficult** it is for a dog to do what we ask – not how good or bad we think he is – and we must pay them accordingly. The rewards we have on offer for our dogs must be something that is valuable to them and that they really want.

We must be prepared to reward them well for doing as we ask – however long it takes and without getting impatient or angry. The longer a dog takes to understand and do as we ask, the more help he needs and greater the reward he deserves for his effort and achievement.

If we become angry instead, he may never learn what we really want him to do. He may also learn to bite us.

Q If your dog is being naughty, is he?

A
a) Doing things to annoy you on purpose?
b) Doing things he enjoys?
c) Having trouble working out what you want him to do?
d) Not being taught properly?
e) Just plain stupid?

(Correct answer on page 68.)

Get your dog used to your life

11

A dog does not need to learn that certain things in the environment are frightening. He does not need something nasty to have happened to him to be afraid of wheelie bins, cars or small children, for example. Being afraid is just the way many dogs automatically feel if they have not met or experienced something before in their lives.

The most important time for dogs to get used to things is when they are puppies, as this is when their brain is best able to learn about the world. What they learn may be both good and bad news and will be remembered for a long time. It is your job to make sure that as many of his new experiences as possible are 'good news'!

The veterinary clinic is one particular environment that young dogs often learn is not only scary but also means something may hurt them. The fact that vets and nurses do not want to hurt any of their patients does not matter to a dog. Extra special care must be taken to make sure that, whenever possible, your puppy has fun and looks forward to being at the vets. Practise asking him to sit wherever you can and take especially tasty treats with you to give him just in case the vet or nurse forgets!

By the time a young dog is six months old, he is the equivalent of a teenager. He must have learnt about almost everything he is expected to cope with later in your life by this age.

There is also no point is getting a dog used to someone else's life. A dog must get used to how **you** live and what **you** expect of him.

If a dog has been brought up on a farm, he may be able to cope with and be friendly towards people in wellington boots, sheep, cows, tractors and his own littermates, but this will not help him with joggers wearing trainers, skateboarders, trains, planes and strange dogs in the park.

Although we think of working dogs, such as sheep dogs and gun dogs, as very clever and well-trained, the pet dogs we have in our houses need to be even better at doing all sorts of different things.

We need our dogs to be happy on their own and happy with lots of people. We need them to tolerate being poked and prodded by show judges and vets. We need them to bark at burglars but not at our friends. We need them to chew **their** toys but not **our** toys. We need them to do exactly what we want them to do but often do not take the time to show them exactly what these things are.

The younger a dog is when he is introduced to all aspects of your life and taught what you need him to do in all situations, the better.

Q What might a dog do if he experiences something he has not come across before in his life?

A a) Try to investigate it?
b) Run away from it?
c) Bark at it?
d) Growl at it?
e) Try to bite it?

(Correct answer on page 69.)

Teach your dog to say 'please'

12

Just as we are taught that it is polite to ask for things that we need and want rather than merely helping ourselves, dogs should also learn that things they want and enjoy in life need to be asked for nicely.

Sometimes they also need to learn to wait a while for things they want, without expecting results immediately. Many dogs have been allowed to think that they can help themselves to anything they want and that the more annoying their behaviour is to us, the better it works in getting our attention!

This is a bad mistake to make.

A very useful doggy equivalent of 'please' is to sit quietly when asked. If from a very young age, a puppy is asked to sit before he is given anything at all that he wants, including games and cuddles as well as bits of food, a 'sit' will become his most useful behaviour – if you like, his 'magic' word!

The word 'sit' can then be used successfully later to stop lots of things that we don't like, such as jumping up, barking and even biting. You can also use it to impress your friends! Just as we say 'please' however old we get, a dog should continue to practise sitting throughout his life.

Equally, we do not expect the word 'please' to only work at certain times and places or even to stop working at all – nor should the 'sit' behaviour.

So, make sure your dog is given something nice for sitting everywhere he goes and whatever else is happening around him. There is no better way to make sure your dog gets used to the world and, at the same time, learns to do as you ask everywhere.

Q How can a dog 'ask nicely' for what he wants?

A
a) Bark for it?
b) Wave a paw?
c) Sit?

(Correct answer on page 69.)

The Ladder of Aggression

Biting

Growling, snapping

Stiffening up, staring

Lying down, leg up

Standing,

Walking away

Turning body away, sitting, pawing

Turning head away

Yawning, blinking, nose licking

The Ladder of Aggression

Because they cannot speak, dogs do many things with their bodies to communicate to companions how they feel and what they want. The main purpose of all the gestures dogs use is to keep the peace. They do not want to have to fight with others any more than you do.

Just as we will try to calm someone down who is upset or angry using words, dog will use their bodies. If a dog raises his paw, puts his ears back or walks away from you when you are upset or angry with him, he is trying to calm you down. Even if you are angry or arguing with someone else, he is likely to behave in exactly the same way as he is now trying to calm both of you down.

Dogs very often seem to us to look as if they know they have done something wrong when we are angry with them. But they do not have the ability to feel guilty as we do. They are instead simply asking us to calm down and stop threatening them. If you continue to be angry with a dog despite his calming attempts, he may begin to feel like growling at you and biting you to make you stop. Whereas you will use words in anger, a dog will use his body language and his teeth.

The Ladder of Aggression is an illustration of many of these gestures. They are used when dogs are in the company of either people or other dogs and they are all designed to try to reduce stress and avert danger, in effect to say, 'Please stay calm!' or even, 'Go away and leave me alone!'. How many of these gestures can you remember being described in the canine commandments and what did they all mean?

The lower rungs on this ladder are the equivalent of polite social gestures that humans use, such as smiling, saying hello, shaking hands, bowing or waving. These are things we do to let other people know we want to be friendly towards them and mean them no harm. We expect similar gestures in return so that we can all remain at ease with people, whether we know them well or not. As long as the response we get is friendly, we learn that smiling, waving and greeting each other politely are good things to do. For dogs, if nose-licking and yawning result in calmness, then a dog learns these are good signals to give as they have the right result.

Biting

Growling, snapping

Stiffening up, staring

Lying down, leg up

Standing, crouched, tail under

Creeping, ears back

Walking away

Turning body away, sitting, pawing

Turning head away

Yawning, blinking, nose licking

55

However, if our smile or wave were to be met with disapproval or anger, it would without doubt start to make us feel upset and rather less like being friendly. Exactly the same is true for dogs. If lower rungs of the ladder do not seem to work, dogs are forced further up towards the top of the ladder and are more likely to growl and bite. Unfortunately, by misunderstanding what a dog is trying to say with his body, we often accidentally make them feel much less friendly towards us.

Getting angry with a dog for walking away from us rather than coming to us, or because he looks guilty about something he has done, will make a dog more likely to move up the ladder. He may even learn to go straight to the top of the ladder immediately just to be on the safe side. Remember above all that a dog who looks 'guilty' or 'sorry', is only asking you to calm down. He is NOT admitting that he has been naughty! The angrier we are and the more a dog tries to calm us down, the more guilty looking he will appear. If we carry on being angry instead of calming down immediately, dogs will learn that the only behaviour which gets people to leave them alone is to bite.

The most useful way to make sure a dog is unlikely to bite you is to ask him to come to you, wherever he is and whether or not he has something in his mouth. If he runs happily towards you, he is saying that he feels safe in your company. It does not necessarily mean he wants a fuss or hug! If, however, he stays lying down, stands still or walks or runs away from you, he is saying the opposite – 'You are threatening me – please stay away!' If you follow him or try to touch him, you will show him that you do not understand his language and make him more likely to have to growl or bite.

None of us would enjoy being misunderstood or being unable to understand what people around us are saying. But this is how many of our dogs feel a lot of the time. Learning to understand what a dog is really trying to say and encouraging him to understand what you mean, but without getting angry, will make both of you very much happier.

Happy dogs have no need to bite.

How to Help Dogs Avoid Going Up Ladders

By Matt Black

Hey! Don't let your dog get madder and madder,
Learn the signs he shows you, like steps on a ladder.

First he offers friendly "Hi there's" and "Hellos",
With blinking or yawning, or licking his nose.

His wish for calm and assurance of harmony,
If misunderstood, will risk acrimony.

He might paw, look away, might climb the first
    step
If he feels your responses are not right, or a threat.

Crouching, creeping and slinking, are next rung
    expressions,
Walking away, he's trying to leave stress situations.

If you ignore these, he'll go on up the
    ladder,
Maybe stand crouched, with tail tucked
    under.

Or he'll lie down, belly up, in a frozen
position,
If he stiffens, and stares, it's fight-time
aggression.

(Of course, not all dogs climb up the steps neatly,
Some dogs ignore certain rungs completely.)

But with all these signs he's letting you know
A fight is not the way he's wanting to go.

So read him, and heed him, or he will not stop
Till he growls* and snaps, climbing rungs to the top.

And his last resort: biting. At all times, it's
for you
To try and learn what he's saying, and know
what to do.

Calm him, talk softly, give him some space
Or a treat, till the fear has gone from his face.

So, for you and your dog to have the best times,
Please learn from the ladder and the steps in these
rhymes.

* Please don't tell your dog off for growling! Like all these signs, growls are your dog telling you, clearly and cleverly, that they are feeling stressed and want the situation to be changed.

The Human Ladder of Aggression

We humans also have what can be thought of as a Ladder of Aggression, where a conversation can escalate from a discussion or minor disagreement to a full-blown argument or even a fight. It may be that you've accidentally upset a friend and need to apologise. Or someone may have upset you and made you feel angry – even by supporting the wrong football team!

Most of us want to fit in and get along with our companions and it is to our advantage to avoid arguments and fights if at all possible. After all, even if you feel you are in the right, is it worth the risk of getting injured in a fight? This is why people of all cultures think it is better to sit down and discuss subjects of disagreement rather than fight about them. This way, we hope to prevent damaging violence.

But even with the best of intentions, we can all lose our temper sometimes and end up arguing and fighting even if we would have preferred not to. Thinking about what we do to settle our upsets and arguments without having to fight may help you see things from a dog's point of view.

Learning objectives

Whole book
- To understand why dogs bite and to stop dogs feeling like biting.
- To realise the importance of human interactions with dogs.
- To realise dogs usually become aggressive to defend themselves and their possessions.
- To understand that there is a graded sequence of gestures, which may culminate in aggression for both dogs and humans.
- To realise that certain actions and situations can trigger aggressive behaviour in both dogs and humans.
- To understand that no dog wants to bite and that dog bites can be avoided.

1   Being cross does not make you the boss
- Dogs have no concept of rank or status.
- Wolves live in families as we do.
- Dogs do not function in 'packs'.
- Training methods based on 'dominance theory' are misguided and dangerous.
- Being angry or violent towards a dog to get your own way is never a good idea. At best, a dog may be confused and think you cannot be trusted and at worst, you may teach the dog to bite you.

2   Any dog may bite if he feels in danger
- Biting is a normal dog behaviour in response to unavoidable threat.
- All dogs, big or small, may bite if the need arises.
- How we behave may make a dog feel threatened and in danger.

The Canine Commandments

- Deliberately threatening a dog in order to train it is not only unkind and unnecessary, but may also be dangerous.

3 Never hit or kick a dog
- We can all lose our temper sometimes and do things we don't mean to.
- If a dog has annoyed you, try not to lose your temper.
- A dog might not forgive you in the future.

4 Never touch a dog you don't know
- Our human need to touch and pet dogs may override common sense.
- Affectionate human actions may be viewed as a threat by a dog.
- If a dog feels threatened, they may bite.

5 Do not tease or deliberately excite a dog
- Over-excited dogs cannot think rationally.
- Excitement is not necessarily the same as happiness.
- An over-excited dog may bite by accident.

6 Dogs do not know the difference between right and wrong
- Dogs have no concept of 'guilt'.
- Dogs are very good at looking 'guilty' if you get angry with them.
- Being angry with a guilty-looking dog will not teach him to be 'good' and may teach him to bite instead.

7 Behaviours that dogs enjoy will be repeated
- All dog training is based on an understanding of what dogs like and dislike.
- It is kinder and safer to train a dog using what it likes rather than using something it finds unpleasant.
- Your appearance and sound like must always predict 'good news' to your dog.

8 Dogs must be taught what you want them to do and they must choose to do it

- Punishing a dog for doing something we think is wrong does not teach him what is right.
- Anything a dog does is his own choice not ours.
- Both dogs and people will be happy if what a dog chooses to do is the same as what we'd like them to do.

9 Do not take anything away from a dog

- Once a dog has something in his mouth, he thinks it's his.
- You will be seen as the thief.
- He may defend his property by growling or even biting.

10 When dogs are being 'bad', they need the most help, not the most punishment

- Dogs being 'bad' are having a hard time getting it right.
- Punishment will only teach them what not to do, not what they should be doing instead.
- If your dog keeps getting things wrong, question whether you are teaching him what is right well enough.

11 Get your dog used to your life

- Dogs do not automatically understand the world around them.
- Anything new may frighten them.
- Dogs are best accustomed to the world when they are young puppies.
- Learning about the world continues for life.

12 Teach your dog to say 'please'

- 'Please' is a word we use to ask politely for something we want. A doggy equivalent is to sit.
- Asking a dog to sit before giving him anything he wants will create a polite dog who is easy to live with.

Answers

1 Being cross does not make you the boss
How do you think you should control a dog?
a) By shouting and scolding if they disobey?
b) By nagging?
c) By asking them nicely?
d) By showing clearly what you want them to do first?

Answer: d
Yes! That's right! Scolding dogs may just teach them to be naughty when you're not there. But once you've shown them clearly what to do and rewarded them for getting it right with plenty of practice, THEN you can ask them nicely with no need for nagging, shouting or scolding.

2 Any dog may bite if he feels in danger
What do you think might make a dog feel frightened and in danger?
a) Fireworks and thunderstorms?
b) Going to the vets and having an injection?
c) Being scolded or smacked?
d) Seeing and hearing people arguing or fighting?
e) Meeting a stranger?

Answer: ALL OF THEM!
All these can make dogs feel frightened. Their first instinct is to run away but if they can't, they might try to make the danger go away by growling and biting.

3 Never hit or kick a dog

Why do you think anyone would hit or kick a dog?

a) They are angry about something the dog has done and lose their temper?

b) They want to stop the dog doing the 'bad' thing again in the future?

c) They are frightened if a dog comes too close to them?

d) For fun?

Answers: I hope no-one would hit or kick a dog for fun! Well done if you gave answer A or B – these are the most common reasons why dogs are hit. But no-one thinks clearly if they are angry and may feel sorry about what they have done later. Nor will dogs learn 'not to do it again'.

But we must also remember answer C. Not everyone is comfortable with dogs and they may be afraid of them. So we shouldn't let our dogs run up to say hello to everyone even if your dog wants to be friendly.

4 Never touch a dog you don't know

What would you do if you saw a dog tied up outside a shop?

a) Go up to stroke and pet the dog?

b) Run past him?

c) Speak to him but keep your distance?

d) Ignore him and walk past slowly?

Answer: c or d

Yes, that's right! Even though you might want to say hello and stroke a dog, you have to think what the dog may want. He may be very friendly and look as if he's pleased to see you. This does not mean he wants a cuddle. He may be sitting calmly and ignoring you. This definitely means he's perfectly happy being left in peace. It is always safer to leave tethered dogs alone and walk calmly past.

The Canine Commandments

5 Do not tease or deliberately excite a dog

How can you tell if a dog wants to play?
a) He runs around with a toy in his mouth?
b) He barks at you while standing over a toy?
c) He's lying in his bed with a toy?

Answer: a or b
Yes, that's right but … it may not be a good idea to play with him whenever he seems to want to. You may end up with a dog who runs around and barks far too much!

Should you try to take a toy away if a dog has it in his bed?

NEVER! He may think you are trying to steal it and think he needs to protect it by growling or snapping. Always call him out of his bed first. If he brings the toy to you and drops it **when you ask**, then you can play with him.

6 Dogs do not know the difference between right and wrong

Do you think a dog knows if he's been bad?
a) Yes
b) No

Answer: b
If you'd said 'yes', why do you think he knows? Because he looks guilty?

A dog does **not** know he's been naughty, only that someone might get cross with him and punish him afterwards. The 'guilty look' misleads many of us into thinking a dog knows he's done wrong.

But the 'guilty look' is a dog's way of trying to calm things down **not** saying he's sorry. Getting angry with a guilty-looking dog may teach him to be afraid of you. He may only run away but you run the risk of him having to growl or snap at you as well.

7 Behaviours that dogs enjoy will be repeated

How do you know when a dog is enjoying himself?
When he is:
a) Chasing a ball?
b) Eating?
c) Chewing his bone?
d) Chewing your shoes?
e) Asleep in his bed?

Answer: ALL OF THEM!
Anything a dog does a lot of means that he finds the activity rewarding. The trick is to make sure that he is rewarded for doing things that are convenient to you and you enjoy too.

8 Dogs must be taught what you want them to do and they must choose to do it

What is the difference between an obedient dog and a well-behaved dog?
a) An obedient dog does what he is told
b) A well-behaved dog is good without being asked
c) No difference

Answer: Now this is a tricky question!
Most grown-ups have not thought about this subject before, so you will have a head-start in understanding dogs! Some dogs may seem accidentally good and get things right most of the time without anyone telling them what to do. These dogs are well-behaved and may also not need very much obedience training.

On the other hand, dogs who are obedient, in other words, good at doing what they are told, may be confused if no-one gives them an instruction and may not be at all well-behaved when left to their own devices.

If you want your dog to be good more of the time, then make sure they are noticed and rewarded whenever they are being good – **whether or not they have been told what to do.**

The Canine Commandments

9 Do not take anything away from a dog
What should you do to make a dog drop what he has in his mouth?
a) Chase and shout at him to leave it?
b) Try and pull it away?
c) Offer him a tasty treat in exchange?
d) Ignore him?

Answer: c or d
Another tricky question! Your answer may well depend on exactly <u>what</u> is in your dog's mouth and how valuable it is to you. But it is never a good idea to chase him, shout or try to pull it away from him and may be dangerous. Offering a treat in exchange for your favourite cap or one of your shoes is the best thing to do.

But dogs often take things that are of no value at all, such as tissue paper, crisp packets or sweet wrappers. In this case, it is best to ignore the dog. If you make a fuss, you may teach your dog that it's exciting to steal things and they'll do it all the more!

10 When dogs are being 'bad', they need the most help, not the most punishment
If your dog is being naughty, is he?
a) Doing things to annoy you on purpose?
b) Doing things he enjoys?
c) Having trouble working out what you want him to do?
d) Not being taught properly?
e) Just plain stupid?

Answer: c, with quite a lot of b and d
Hardly any dogs are stupid, and they certainly do not do things to annoy us on purpose, but they may well be having fun when they run off with one of our shoes or raid the rubbish bin. Some dogs do have more difficulty learning what we want them to do than others. Or could it be that sometimes we are not very good teachers?

If a dog keeps on doing the wrong thing, we first have to ask ourselves if we've ever properly taught him what is right?

11 Get your dog used to your life
What might a dog do if he experiences something he has not come across before in his life?
a) Try to investigate it?
b) Run away from it?
c) Bark at it?
d) Growl at it?
a) Try to bite it?

Answer: ALL OF THEM!
From a dog's point of view, it is always safer to be wary of anything novel. More confident dogs may be brave enough to try to investigate someone or something new. But more timid dogs may think that running away is the safest thing to do. If a dog cannot run away, then they may try to get the scary thing or person to go away instead by barking or growling. If all else fails, they may try to bite.

The younger a dog is when meeting unfamiliar people and things, the better. But whatever their age, make sure something nice happens whenever your dog is introduced to anything new. The best way is to give your dog a tasty food treat!

12 Teach your dog to say 'please'
How can a dog 'ask nicely' for what he wants?
a) Bark for it?
b) Wave a paw?
c) Sit?

Answer: I hope you all said c – to sit!

Often dogs learn that barking gets them what they want – to go out into the garden to play or have a wee for example. This may seem convenient to begin with, but a dog that barks for everything he wants can become very annoying. Waving a paw can easily change into scratching at things in a demanding way.

A calm 'sit' should become a dog's most valuable behaviour – his 'magic word'!

Glossary

aggression – threatening behaviour that all animals, including humans, may use if they themselves, or things they value, are threatened. All aggression is potentially damaging.

barking – a noise dogs make with their mouths open to communicate to others. They have many different barks for different purposes.

commandment – an instruction that someone else, who knows more than you do, thinks is a good idea.

dangerous – something that might be harmful to us.

disobedient or 'naughty' dog – one who chooses to do something other than what we want.

dog bite – an expression of aggression where a dog's teeth make contact with the skin of another individual.

domestic dog – a species of animal evolved from the same ancestor as the wolf. All modern-day wolves and dogs have descended from the same common ancestor.

environment – everything and everyone around us, wherever we are.

growling – a low rumble a dog will make if it feels threatened or in danger. It is an expression of aggression and a warning to stay away.

guilt – the feeling you have when you know you have done something wrong.

The Canine Commandments

ignoring – not approaching, looking at or paying any attention at all to something.

obedient or 'good' dog – one who chooses to do what we want them to do when we ask them.

politeness – behaving in a way which puts other people, and dogs, at ease.

punishment – something unpleasant designed to stop behaviour we don't like.

reward – something pleasant designed to encourage behaviour we do like.

snap – an expression of aggression when a dog's teeth snap shut close to, but do not make contact with, the skin of another individual.

well-behaved dog – one who chooses to do what we want them to do without being asked.

Further reading and resources

Canine Behaviour in Mind: Applying Behavioural Science to Our Lives with Dogs, Suzanne Rogers (ed.), 5m Books, 2022

Demystifying Dog Behaviour for Veterinarians, Kendal Shepherd, Taylor & Francis, 2021

Dog Bites: A Multidisciplinary Perspective, D. S. Mills and C. Westgarth, 5m Books, 2017

Dog Is Love, Clive Wynne, Quercus Publishing, 2019

'English hospital episode data analysis (1998–2018) reveal that the rise in dog bite hospital admissions is driven by adult cases', Tulloch, J. et al., www.nature.com/scientificreports (2021) 11:1767

'How many people have been bitten by dogs? A cross-sectional survey of prevalence, incidence and factors associated with dog bites in a UK community', Westgarth, C., et al., J Epidemiol Community Health (2018) 72:331–336

In Defence of Dogs, John Bradshaw, Allen Lane, 2011

'Keeping ourselves safe near dogs', Association for the Study of Animal Behaviour educational resources, www.asab.org/educationprimary

Sniffing Lamp-posts – Poetry Inspired by Dogs, Matt Black, Upside Down Books, 2020 (Copies available from www.matt-black.co.uk with proceeds going to the Dog's Trust, and Coventry Dog Rescue.)

The Canine Commandments

The Culture Clash, Jean Donaldson, James & Kenneth Publishers, 1996

The Happy Dog Owner, Cari Westgarth, Wellbeck Publishing, 2021

The Science Behind a Happy Dog: Canine Training, Thinking and Behaviour, E. Grigg and T. Donaldson, 5m Books, 2017

Follow-up questionnaire

Kendal and we at 5m hope very much that you enjoyed this book and would really like to know how you got on with it: whether you understood the book, if you found the commandments easy to follow and, most importantly, whether they have helped you get along with dogs – either your own or other people's.

If you feel able to give us some feedback (for better or worse!) please go to the 5m website and follow the Canine Commandments link to a short survey.

www.5mbooks.com/product/the-canine-commandments-2nd-edition